JASMI[illegible]
LAUNCHES A STARTUP

entrepreneurship books for kids

Author : Bachar Karroum
Illustrator : Jesus Vazquez Prada

ISBN: 978-1-988779-02-7

Dépôt légal : bibliothèque et archives nationales du Québec, 2018.
Dépôt légal : bibliothèque et archives Canada, 2018.

Author: **Bachar Karroum**
Illustrator: **Jesus Vazquez Prada**
Graphic Designer: **Samuel Gabriel**
Cover Designer: **German Creative**
Editor: **Aline Massouh**
Proofreader: **Christina Cutting**

To my lovely daughter Jasmine!

Jasmine is a smart little girl who loves to help those in need. One day, while visiting her friend at the hospital, Jasmine was disturbed by what she saw.

She noticed unhappiness in the eyes of the sick children.

This made her feel so sad.

At home, Jasmine could not stop thinking about those kids.

Suddenly, she came up with an incredible idea.

Inspired by her father's business, Jasmine wondered if she could start a company to help them. But, what to do and where to begin? Jasmine had no idea. She decided to seek out her father's advice.

Jasmine presented her idea to dad, and the problem she wanted to solve.

"That's an excellent idea, Jasmine!" said Dad.

He encouraged her to start, take risks, and move into action.

"You should also consider finding friends to work with," added Dad.

The next day, Jasmine tried to convince her classmates to build a team. Unfortunately, nobody was interested.

Disappointed, she started to think about alternatives.

“I will not give up,” shouted Jasmine.

Later that day, her cousin Clara came over for a visit.

Excited, Jasmine decided to share her idea with Clara.

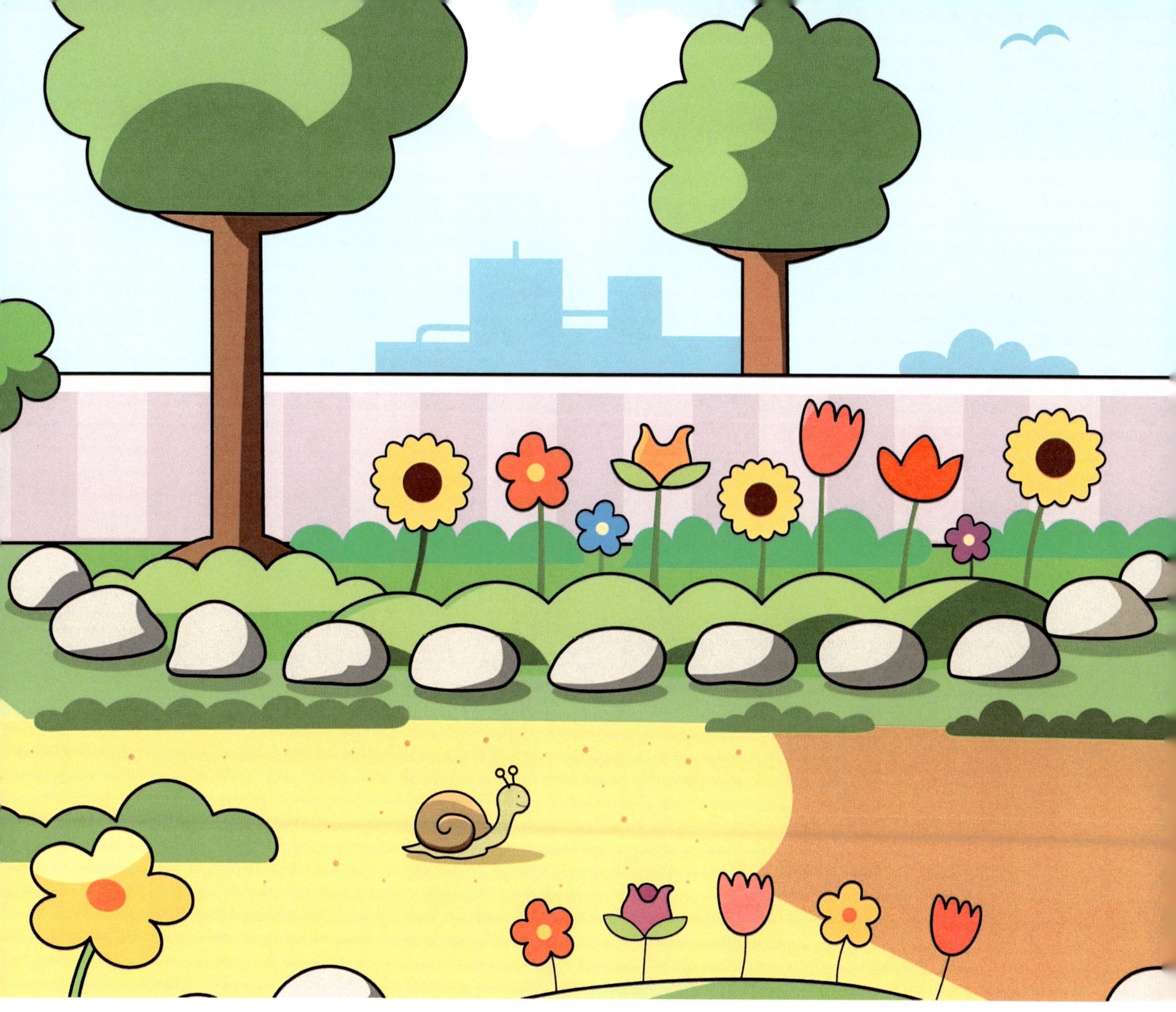

"What a great idea, I love it," said Clara.

She agreed to work with Jasmine and both girls started planning.

Without losing time, the two cousins started executing their plan. Jasmine grabbed some pens, pencils, and a pair of scissors. Clara found a set of stationery. “Hope you get better soon!” wrote Jasmine.

“Stay strong. You will soon feel well!” jotted down Clara.

Can you guess Jasmine’s business idea?

A company that creates and distributes get-well cards!

During the weekend, the girls' parents drove them to the hospital to deliver their first set of cards. Jasmine and Clara walked into the rooms and gave out the cards to the children.

Much to their surprise, the children did not seem to really like the cards. Confused, they decided to ask the children how they felt about receiving the cards. What could be done to bring a smile to their faces?

Back home, now aware of what the problem was, they started adapting the cards to the kids' needs. Jasmine and Clara worked very hard...

...adding colour, characters, making the cards more interesting and fun.

The girls were determined to make the sick children smile.

The next weekend, the two cousins went back to the hospital with the new batch of cards in hand.

Success! The sick kids' pale faces started to brighten—they were happy and smiling. Jasmine and Clara were proud of their achievement.

Motivated, the girls wanted to bring more cheer cards to other hospitals.

"But we need help to do the job," said Jasmine.

"Yes, let's ask for help," confirmed Clara.

Jasmine and Clara came up with another great idea.

They decided to present their project during Show and Tell at school and ask for help.

The next day, Clara joined Jasmine's class for the Show and Tell, and the cousins presented their work. Realizing that the project was serious, many students volunteered to help create more cards.

"What a wonderful project," said the teacher.

She offered to send flyers to the students' home, asking parents if they would like to contribute and buy extra supplies.

Over the next few days after school, the art teacher met with all the volunteer kids. The cousins suggested that they divide the group into two teams.

Everyone was given a job, and together they created many, many beautiful cards. The first batch of cards was soon ready for distribution.

The following weekend, parents volunteered to drive the students to the hospitals. The sick children's faces brighten up as soon as they opened the cards.

Everyone was proud to see how their creations made a difference. Jasmine's new team worked well together, and their hard work truly paid off. Such great team spirit and wonderful accomplishment!

"We did it!" shouted Jasmine and Clara.

With focus, determination and a positive attitude, everything is possible.

The whole team came together for a group hug and promised to keep working together.

Important to read to your kids!

When Jasmine started her company, she had a real problem to solve. She wanted to change the sad feelings of the sick children. Her passion for helping those in need was a big motivator.

The target market was the children at the hospital. With all the doubts she had, Jasmine sought out advice from people with more experience, such as her father. Then she decided to take a risk and move into action.

At the beginning, the job was not easy because it was hard to find support from her classmates. Jasmine did not give up, and soon her cousin Clara joined her team.

The product they decided to create, to raise the spirits of the sick children, was get-well cards. At first, this product was not perfect but after speaking with their customers, they were able to improve the cards and transform the project into a real success.

Then the two girls faced money and human resource problems when they realized they needed to increase the production of their cards.

Creatively, Jasmine and Clara found a solution to their problem. They called for volunteers to finance the materials, market to other hospitals, create more products, and distribute the new batches of cards. Working with a team was very helpful. It was fun, the team spirit was positive, and everyone was motivated.

The whole team of adults and children were focused on their plan and determined to succeed. Together, they kept an eye on the main problem: how to make the sick kids smile again.

Never forget that if there is a will, there is a way!

Made in the USA
Columbia, SC
16 September 2021